DRUMMER'S GUIDE TO FILLS

PETE SWEENEY

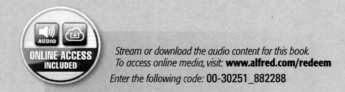

Stream or download the audio content for this book.
To access online media, visit: **www.alfred.com/redeem**
Enter the following code: **00-30251_882288**

Audio recorded by Mark Schane-Lydon at WorkshopLive.com, Pittsfield, MA

Cover photograph: © JUPITERIMAGES/ Creatas / Alamy

Alfred

Alfred Music
P.O. Box 10003
Van Nuys, CA 91410-0003
alfred.com

ISBN-10: 0-7390-5270-5 (Book & Online Audio)
ISBN-13: 978-0-7390-5270-9 (Book & Online Audio)

TABLE OF CONTENTS

ABOUT THE AUTHOR

PHOTO COURTESY OF PETE SWEENEY

Pete Sweeney has been a professional musician since 1983. He studied with Dave Calarco and Joe Morello, and attended the Drummers Collective in New York City.

Pete has been a faculty member at the National Guitar Workshop since 1993. He has performed with many great musicians such as "Dangerous" Dan Toler, Duke Robillard, Mick Goodrick, Larry Coryell, Nick Brignola, Cary DeNigris, and Frank Gambale. He has performed concerts with Robben Ford, Andy Summers (of the Police), and Laurel Masse (of the Manhattan Transfer). Pete has also performed on two Grammy-nominated CDs with Jay Traynor and the Joey Thomas Big Band, and can be heard on the soundtrack of the Miramax film *The Castle*.

Pete Sweeney endorses Mapex drums, Aquarian drum heads, Vic Firth drum sticks, and Sabian cymbals. He can be contacted via e-mail at P9565@aol.com, and you can check out his website at www.petesweeney.net.

ACKNOWLEDGEMENTS

I would like to thank Nat Gunod and Dave Smolover at the National Guitar Workshop. Thanks to Neil Larrivee at Vic Firth; Bob Boos and Paul Celucci at Sabian; Chris Brady and Roy Burns at Aquarian; and Joe Hibbs and Jeff Ivester at Mapex. Thanks to my parents Patrick and Patricia Sweeney, my brother Paul, and niece Lacee. Special thanks to Tobias Ralph and Ian Carroll for their input. I would like to thank my teachers Dave Calarco and Joe Morello for their insight and inspiration. Thanks also to Burgess Speed, Tim Phelps, Matthew Liston, and Mark Schane-Lydon at Workshop Arts for their help on this book. Lastly, I would like to thank Victoria Cipollari for everything!

0

0

A

Online audio is included with this book. Use the recordings to help ensure you're capturing the feel of the examples, interpreting the rhythms correctly, and so on. The symbol shown at the top left appears next to every example that is on the recording. The number indicates which track corresponds to the example you want to hear. If there's a decimal (1.1, 1.2, etc.), it means that there's more than one example on the track. Many of the examples are divided into multiple variations, indicated with a letter (A, B, C, etc.). If the variation is included on the recording, it will be indicated with a small speaker symbol (bottom left).

INTRODUCTION

Hello and welcome to the *Drummer's Guide to Fills!* This book is intended to help you play musical fills and solos on the drumset. Whether you are a beginner or have been playing music for years, you will find many fun and challenging musical examples in this book. We will take a step-by-step approach so that each concept is clearly understood. You will be given lots of variations to work on, and drum fills to suit your needs in any style of music—whether it's rock, funk, jazz, or Latin. Also included are some valuable exercises that can be used as warm-ups for your hands and feet around the drumset. Let's begin by answering a few questions:

What is a drum fill?

Drum fills are one of the most misunderstood aspects of drumset playing. A drum fill, in the most basic sense, is a part of a song where the drummer plays a variation of the groove that leads the music into another section of the song. In popular music, the sections of a song are usually divided up like this:

> *Verse:* The main melodic section of a song. This is the part of the song that usually tells a story. It can also be called a *stanza.*

> *Bridge:* A transitional section. Many times, the bridge will serve as transition from the verse to the chorus.

> *Chorus:* The section that summarizes the main idea of the song, often with a catchy melody that makes you want to sing along. The chorus is often referred to as the *refrain.* Many times, the title of the song is contained in the lyrics of this section.

The drummer may play a figure or musical phrase that leads the band into these sections in a way that is musically complementary. This is what is commonly called a drum fill. In pop and rock music, these drum fills are usually short in duration. They are intended to give the music a lift into the next section.

Another kind of drum fill is when the drummer sets up a musical phrase. These are sometimes referred to as *hits* or *shots.* These hits are part of a musical arrangement where everyone in the band is landing on the same note. The drummer can lead the other musicians into this hit by playing a well-timed drum fill in the appropriate space. Check any big band recording to hear examples of this type of playing.

What's the difference between a fill and a solo?

Generally speaking, a drum *fill* is shorter in duration than a drum *solo*. A fill is a musical phrase that often connects one section of a song to another, whereas a solo may be a whole section of a song where the drummer is featured. Fills and solos are very similar in the sense that they may share the same rhythmic vocabulary; the basic components are very much the same.

How do I develop better fills on the drumset?

This is a question I get asked a lot as a private instructor. The short answer is to immerse yourself in the language of music and really study your instrument. By studying music, you will become more familiar with chord movement and song structure. If you were to play piano, guitar, or bass, you would have to know all of the basic elements of music applied to the songs you are playing. As a drummer, you must also be aware of these aspects so that your playing compliments the music at the appropriate times. Knowing the basic song structure helps you do this. Knowing the basics of music can also help you communicate with other musicians and make better musical decisions.

You must also study your instrument. Get to know the history of the great drummers who have contributed to the evolution of music. Listen to their recordings and learn some of their musical vocabulary. There are great drummers and classic recordings in every style of music. In order to play good-sounding drum fills, spend some time learning fills by drummers you admire. This will help you build a vocabulary you can use for your own fills.

Another way to play better fills is to understand and practice different musical concepts that will help you become a better improviser. Concepts such as theme, variation, repetition, melodic lines, stickings, odd phrasings, etc. will help create a foundation for you to create your own unique-sounding fills. The key here is to understand the process, rather than just merely copying licks.

Playing drum fills is one of the most enjoyable aspects of playing the drumset! However, there are some pitfalls to be aware of. Often, inexperienced drummers will play a great groove, only to lose the beat while playing a fill. They may speed up or slow down during a fill or may come out too early or too late. This results in a less-than-desirable outcome! With consistent practice and dedication, you can play amazing drum fills.

CHAPTER ONE
MUSIC TERMINOLOGY AND NOTE VALUES

In this chapter, we'll take a look at the most frequently used symbols for notating music. You can read through this now, or refer to it later if you come across notation you do not understand.

THE STAFF

Music is written on a *staff* of five lines and four spaces. The symbol at the beginning of the staff in the left-hand corner is called a *percussion clef.* Each line and space represents a different instrument on the drumset.

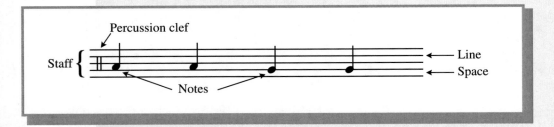

DRUMSET NOTATION KEY

The notation key below shows how the different instruments of the drumset are represented on the percussion staff. You will want to refer to this key if you have any questions regarding notation in this book.

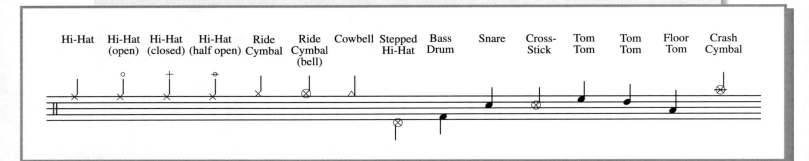

MEASURES

Beats are the most basic unit of musical time. They are grouped into *measures* of equal length, that is, each measure contains the same number of beats. Measures are marked with vertical *barlines.* Short sections end with a *double barline.*

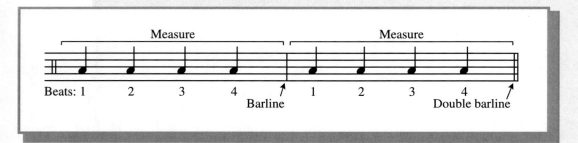

THE REPEAT SIGN

A *repeat* means to go back to the beginning and play again.

Repeat sign

TIME SIGNATURE

At the beginning of every musical piece is a *time signature.* The top number tells you how many beats are in a measure. The bottom number tells you what kind of note gets one beat.

$\dfrac{4}{4}$ = Four beats in a measure
= The quarter note gets one beat

$\dfrac{5}{8}$ = Five beats in measure
= The eighth note gets one beat

DIFFERENT STYLES OF DRUM NOTATION

There are many different styles of drum notation. The style used most often in this book shows the stems of all the notes going up. In most cases, this is the clearest representation of the rhythms.

However, that same phrase can be written with the stems for the hands going up and the stems for the feet going down, like this:

This shows a clear separation of parts and can be very useful as well.

TEMPO MARKINGS

This equation gives the speed or tempo of the exercise. For example, the marking $\quarternote = 120$ indicates that the quarter notes should be played at 120 beats-per-minute (bpm).

ACCENT MARK

An *accent* mark $>$ above a note means to emphasize (make louder) that particular note.

ADDITIONAL REPEAT SIGNS

This repeat sign means to repeat the previous measure:

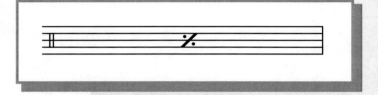

This one means to repeat the previous two measures:

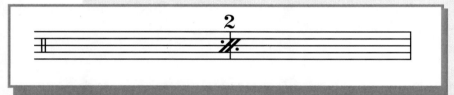

DYNAMIC MARKINGS

A *dynamic marking* next to a note indicates at what volume the phrase should be played. Here is a list of some of the most commonly used makings.

Pianissimo (*pp*)	Very soft
Piano (*p*)	Soft
Mezzo Piano (*mp*)	Moderately soft
Mezzo Forte (*mf*)	Moderately loud
Forte (*f*)	Loud
Fortissimo (*ff*)	Very loud

NOTE VALUES: DUPLE

Here are some of the basic note values and their corresponding *rests*. The rest is a silent note that is counted but not played. The following note values are all evenly divided, or *duple*, rhythms.

A *whole note* lasts for four beats, and it takes up a whole measure in $\frac{4}{4}$ time.

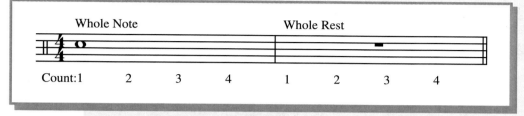

A *half note* lasts for two beats and takes up half a measure.

A *quarter note* lasts for one beat and takes up a quarter of a measure.

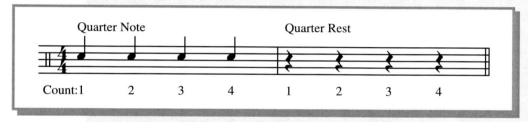

Eighth notes last for half a beat. If you divide a quarter note in half, you get eighth notes. They are counted "1–&–2–&–3–&–4–&."

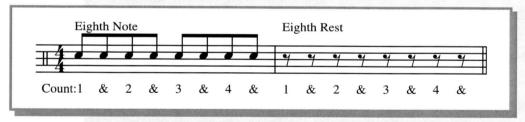

There are four evenly-spaced *sixteenth notes* in the duration of one beat. They are counted "1–e–&–a–2–e–&–a–3–e–&–a–4–e–&–a."

Thirty-second notes are twice as fast as sixteenth notes. There are eight thirty-second notes in the duration of one beat. They are not typically counted individually, due to their short duration. It's best to keep the sixteenth-note count going ("1–e–&–a" etc.) and play two notes per count.

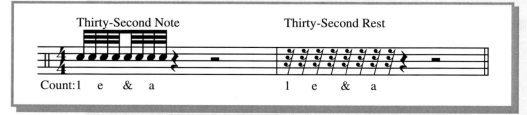

TRIPLET NOTE VALUES

Eighth-note triplets consist of three evenly spaced notes in the time of one beat. They can be counted "1–&–a–2–&–a–3–&–a–4–&–a."

Sixteenth-note triplets are six evenly spaced notes in the time of one beat. They are twice as fast as eighth note triplets.

NOTE VALUE TABLE

This table shows you the relationship between the basic note values.

TIED NOTES

A *tie* is used to connect two notes. Play the first note and let it last for the duration of the two notes combined.

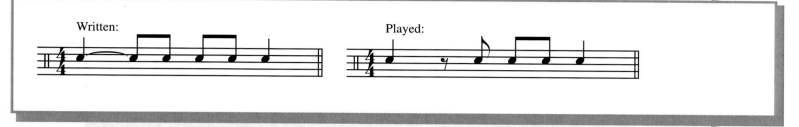

DOTTED NOTES

A *dot* after a note means to increase the note's value by one half. For instance, a dotted quarter note is worth one and a half beats. A dotted eighth note is worth an eighth note plus one sixteenth.

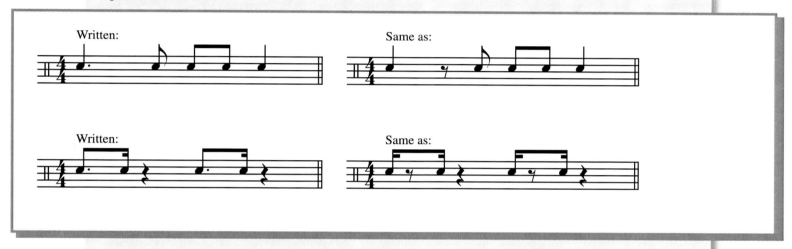

LONG AND SHORT NOTES

Often, you will see notation indicating not only the rhythm of a musical passage, but the length or duration as well. Here's a figure written one way:

Here's the same rhythm written with the second note having a longer duration.

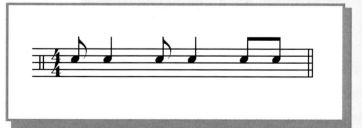

So, these two variations will sound the same because the sound of the drums trail off quickly after they are struck, unlike melodic instruments that can hold notes for longer durations. The function of notation is to make the music as easy to read and understand as possible. So, in this book, either variation may be used for any particular example, depending on which one represents the musical ideas more clearly.

CHAPTER TWO
HAND PATTERNS

In this chapter, we'll take a look at some of the most important hand patterns, or *stickings*, that are used on the drumset. By studying these stickings, you will greatly increase your ability to play more advanced ideas in your drum fills and solos. Let's start with some basic roll patterns: the *single-stroke roll* and the *double-stroke roll*. If you are left-handed, please reverse all of the stickings and start with the left hand.

Single-Stroke Roll

R = Right Hand
L = Left Hand

Double-Stroke Roll

The *paradiddle* is a combination of both the single- and double-stroke rolls. Make sure you memorize the sticking pattern.

Paradiddle

This exercise combines all three hand patterns. Observe the stickings and listen for evenness of the hands.

Combination Exercise

SIXTEENTH-NOTE HAND PATTERNS

The following exercises are essential hand patterns using sixteenth notes. Practice these slowly at first and strive for evenness of the hands. After you have the basic stickings memorized, increase the tempo. You should practice these exercises with a *metronome* or *drum machine* (electronic devices that provide a steady beat at a tempo of your choice); this will help you with accurate spacing of your notes.

Single Stroke

Double Stroke

Paradiddles

MIXED STICKINGS WITH SIXTEENTH NOTES

The next series of exercises will introduce you to combinations of single and double strokes. These are great for gaining control with the sticks and will give you lots of options for playing drum fills and solos.

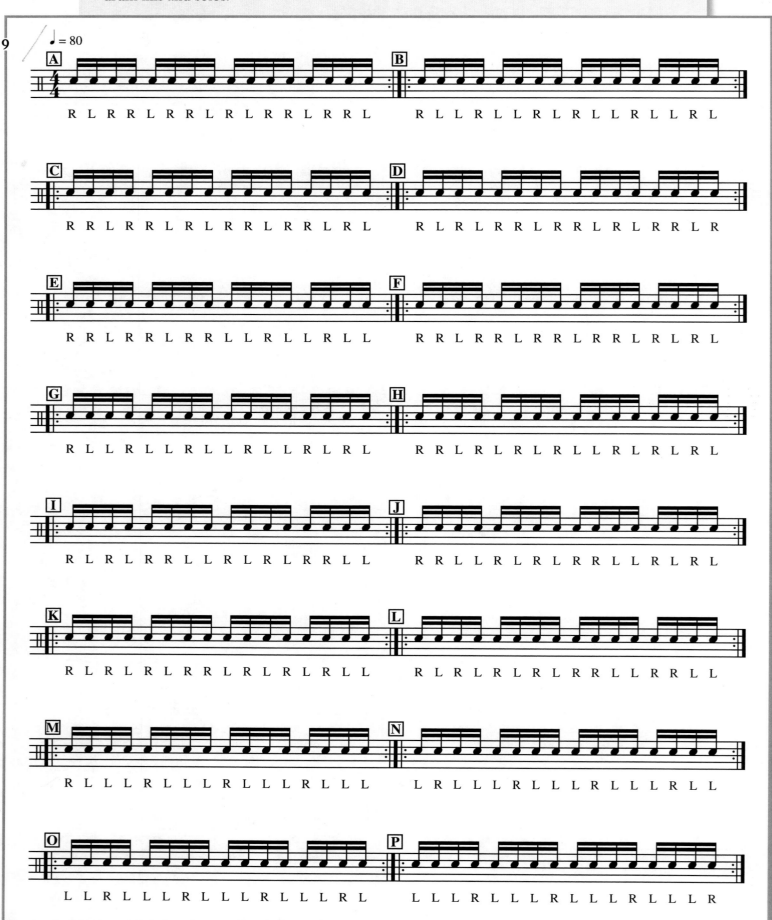

TRIPLET HAND PATTERNS

Here are some examples that use triplets. Practice these exercises slowly at first and concentrate on memorizing the sticking. Also, listen for evenness of the hands.

Single Stroke

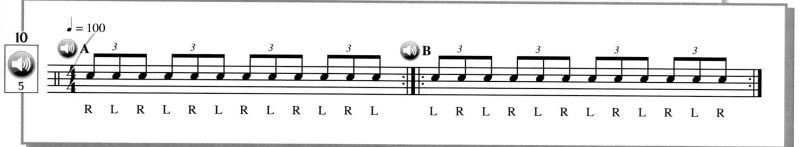

Double Stroke

Mixed Stickings

Double Paradiddle

A *double paradiddle* is a paradiddle with a repeated (or doubled) single-stroke element.

ACCENTS

One of the most important ways to increase your musicality on the drumset is to use *accented* notes. This simply means that you will play certain notes of a musical passage louder, with emphasis. Let's start with a single-stroke roll using sixteenth notes, and we'll accent the very first note of each group of four.

Now, play the bass drum on all four beats and play the same hand pattern on the snare drum. The bass drum should lock right in with the accents being played on the right hand.

Since there are four potential places where a single sixteenth note can be accented in one beat (1–e–&–ah), you will need to practice and become very familiar with each spot. The following series of exercises will help you to do that. Notice that the bass drum does not line up with the accents (except in Example D). Your right hand will be playing on the first and third sixteenths of each beat, and your left plays the second and fourth. Take your time and practice this accurately.

The next step will be to accent groups of two successive sixteenth notes. The bass drum playing quarter notes will act as a consistent timing guide.

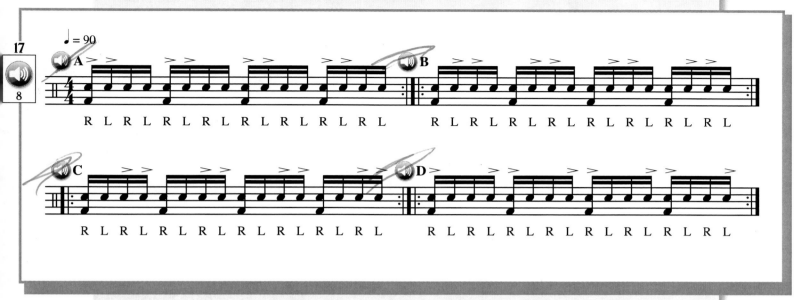

TRIPLET ACCENTS

Here are some examples to work on that use the triplet note value. Use a single-stroke roll sticking throughout. Continue to play the bass drum on all four quarter notes.

PRACTICE IDEAS WITH THE HAND PATTERNS

The purpose of the hand patterns is to get you prepared for playing some of the more complex movements around the drumset. Using different stickings opens up possibilities and new options as you are playing fills. For instance, start with this sticking pattern:

Then, play it between two drums, and it will sound like this:

Here are some other applications around the set:

This process of drumset orchestration can be done with any of the stickings found in this chapter. Use your imagination and experiment with orchestrating a basic pattern around the set. Here's another hand pattern with some drumset orchestration.

CHAPTER THREE
HAND AND FOOT COORDINATION STUDIES

In this chapter, we'll focus on a series of exercises that will greatly increase the coordination between your hands and feet. This kind of interplay is essential for playing drum fills and solos that incorporate the bass drum as well as the hands. Start off slowly and strive for an even sound between your snare and bass drum. You may want to practice these with a metronome or drum machine to help with rhythmic accuracy.

Sixteenth-Note Ideas

ADDING THE HI-HAT

After you become comfortable with these exercises, it's a good idea to play the hi-hats with your left foot stepping on quarter notes. This will add another dimension to your coordination and give a strong quarter-note pulse throughout.

HI-HAT SUBSTITUTION

You may also want to substitute what you are playing on the bass drum for the stepped hi-hat. This is great for working on your four-way coordination.

EIGHTH-NOTE TRIPLET HAND AND FOOT COMBINATIONS

Now, let's work on coordinating the hands and feet with triplet rhythms. These studies are essential for playing fills in jazz and blues music, which use triplets as their primary rhythmic basis.

HAND AND FOOT WARM-UP EXERCISES

It's important to warm up your hands and feet to increase your sense of coordination and fluidity at the drumset. The following series of exercises will provide a challenging warm-up and a foundation for many of the drum fills and solo ideas that follow. Take your time and practice these accurately.

CHAPTER FOUR
GETTING STARTED WITH DRUM FILLS

PRACTICE FORMS

Before we start playing drum fills, it is very important to work on some musical forms to which they can be applied. Most popular music is based on two-, four-, and eight-measure structures. Below is an example of a two-measure rock beat. Notice how the second measure is slightly different than the first. This is a basic example of *theme and variation*.

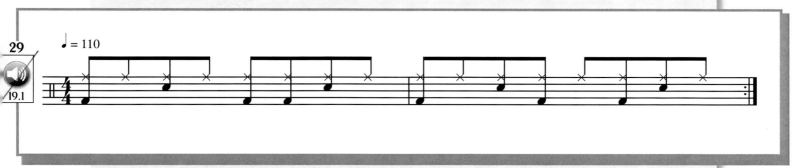

Let's take the same idea and mark the beginning of this two-measure form with a crash cymbal on beat 1.

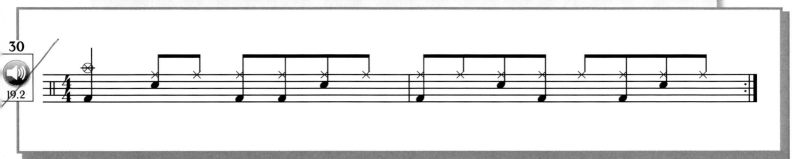

Here's the same idea applied to a four-measure structure.

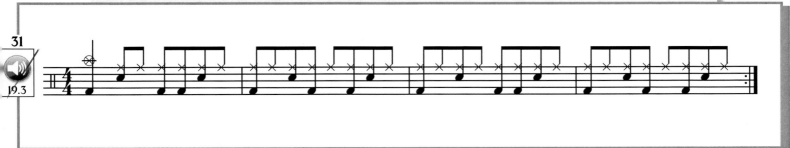

And finally, here's the same idea applied to an eight-measure structure.

COUNTING MEASURES

It is really important to count the measures within these musical forms. You will need to know exactly where you are bar-wise in the structure to be able to apply fills in the correct place. Here's a method that allows you to play a four-measure form and count the beats and the measures.

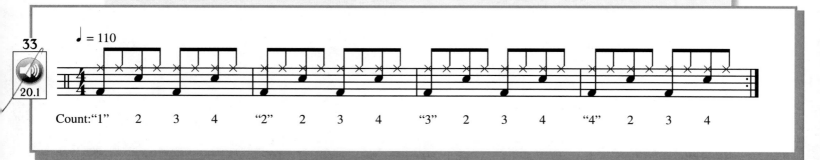

Count: "1" 2 3 4 "2" 2 3 4 "3" 2 3 4 "4" 2 3 4

Once you become familiar with this, you may only need to count the measures.

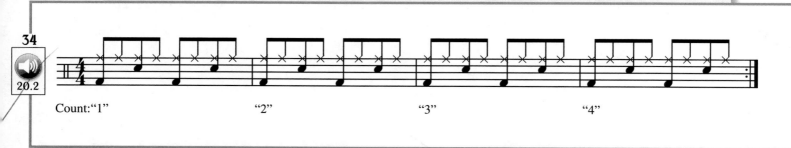

Count: "1" "2" "3" "4"

Practice counting four measures while playing some of your favorite beats. This will help you to internalize the overall musical structure. Eventually, with practice, this will become second nature. If we apply this concept to an eight-measure idea, it will look like this.

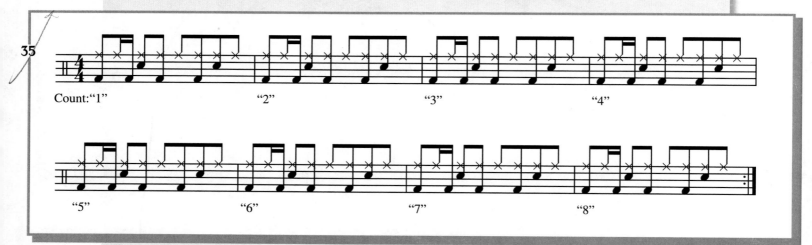

Count: "1" "2" "3" "4"

"5" "6" "7" "8"

GROOVE FILLS

Now that you are familiar with counting bars, let's begin to play some drum fills that are variations of the groove. These are fills that are easy to play and work well musically because they fit into the basic time feel you are playing. Your right hand continues to play eighth notes as you play the groove fill. These examples will be based on a four-measure structure. The fill or groove variation will be played on the fourth measure.

MORE GROOVE FILLS

In these examples, we will focus on some groove fills that use sixteenth notes. This is a great way to break up the time in a rock or funk setting.

GROOVE FILLS WHILE PLAYING THE RIDE CYMBAL

A great way to break up the time in a song is by going over to the ride cymbal. While you are on the ride, you can add some other drums into the groove fills with your left hand. The following examples are written as two-measure ideas, with the groove in the 1st measure and the fill in the 2nd measure. These can and should be practiced in four- and eight-measure structures as well.

ONE-MEASURE EIGHTH-NOTE FILLS

Here are some basic ideas for playing eighth-note drum fills that are one measure in length.
Make sure you count as you are practicing these so that you are really accurate with the fills.
All of these examples will be condensed into a two-measure structure.

Here are some more ideas for eighth-note drum fills that move around the drumset, using different tom toms.

MELODIC BASIS FOR FILLS

Drum fills are easier to understand if you consider they are really embellishments of a basic skeletal phrase. For instance, take a look at this next example: the basic melodic phrase consists of quarter notes that are orchestrated around the drumset.

Now, add eighth notes while still maintaining the basic melodic phrase around the drums.

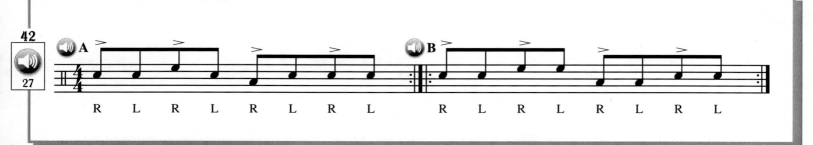

Here's another simple idea using quarter notes:

Now, converted into eighth notes, it might sound like this:

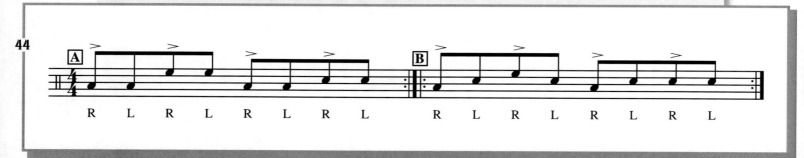

MORE MELODIC IDEAS

The following examples will provide you with more ideas for eighth-note drum fills. First, play the basic melodic idea, then play it as a complete drum fill. When you improvise drum fills in a musical setting, it's important to hear a basic phrase on which you can base the fill. This will make your drum fills flow better and be more musical.

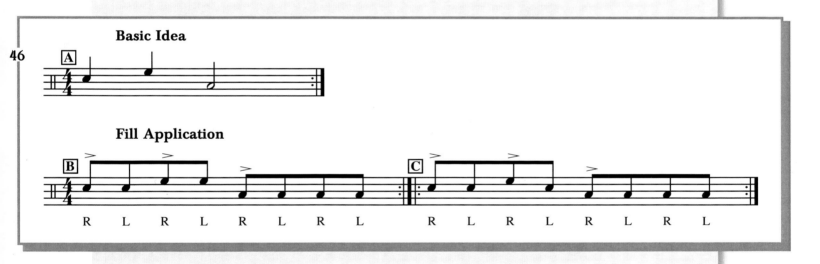

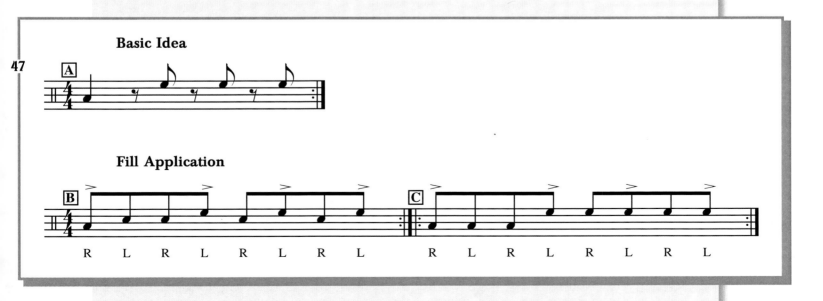

USING THE BASS DRUM IN FILLS

A very cool way to play fills is by using the bass drum as a "third hand." This is where all of the previous coordination studies are really helpful. Make sure that all of the fills are accurate. Be sure to count as you are practicing!

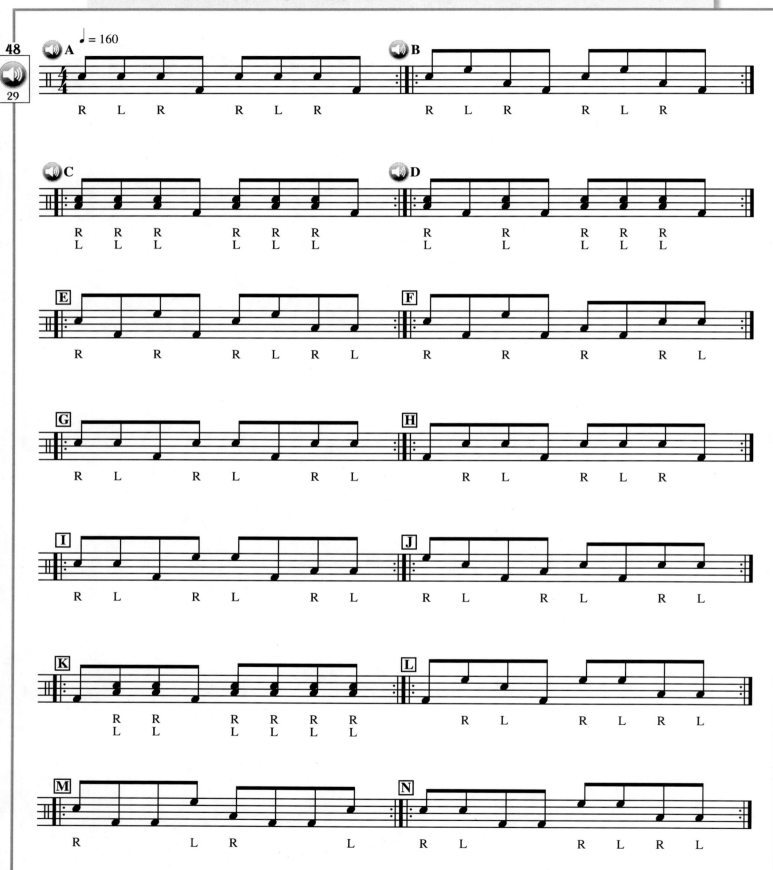

CHAPTER FIVE
SIXTEENTH-NOTE DRUM FILLS

BUILDING BLOCKS

The next series of exercises will give you the ability to execute sixteenth notes in various groupings. This is a necessary skill in order to accurately play the following drum fills that use broken up sixteenth notes. Make sure you use a metronome and count as you practice these exercises. All of the broken sixteenth-note groupings should be practiced initially with a quarter-note bass drum to provide a steady time reference.

Single-Note Sixteenths

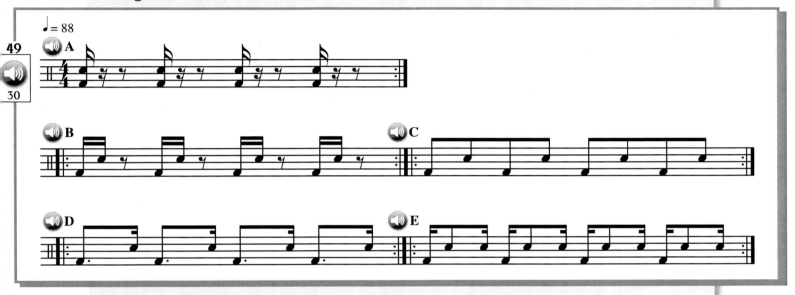

Two-Note Sixteenths

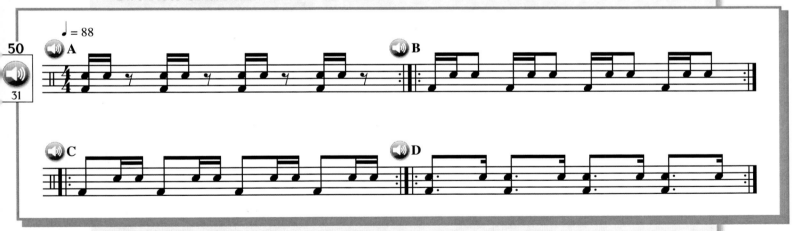

Three-Note Sixteenths

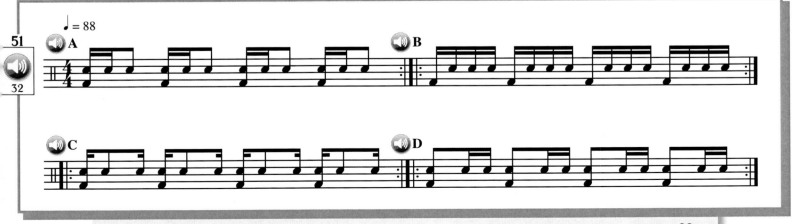

COMBINATION STUDY WITH SIXTEENTH NOTES

Now, practice combining the previous sixteenth-note groupings. Take your time and work at this accurately. You may wish to practice only one measure at a time until each measure is fully understood. Play all of these examples with a quarter-note bass drum. Eventually, practice them without the bass drum, but still count the sixteenth notes.

52

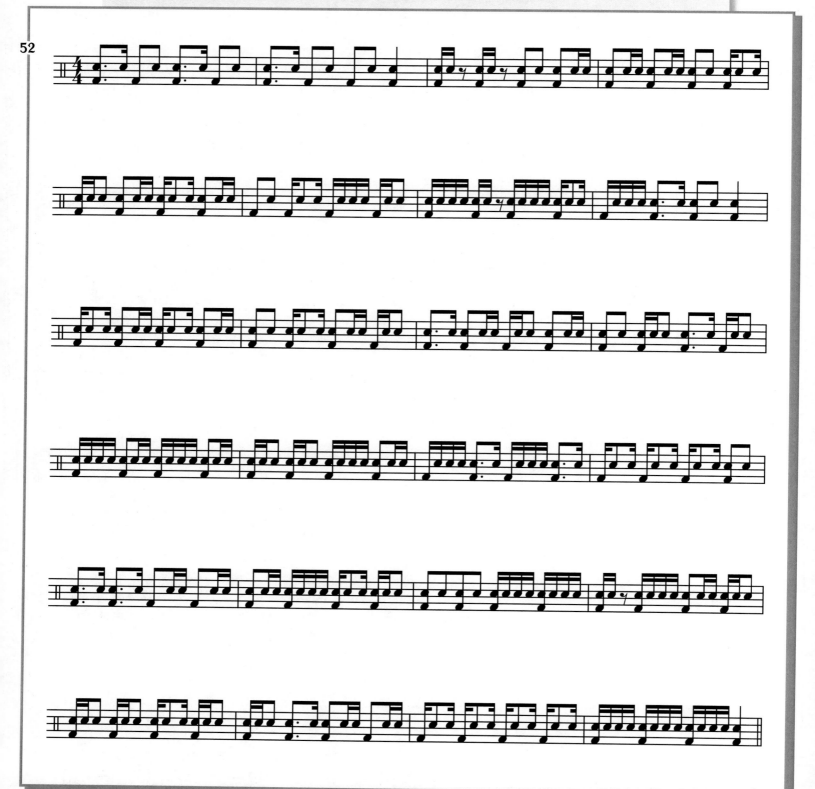

ONE-BEAT SIXTEENTH-NOTE DRUM FILLS

Let's get started playing some sixteenth-note fills at the drumset. We will begin by playing fills that are one beat in duration and that occur at the end of the measure. This is very common in rock and funk music. All examples are written using a two-measure structure but can and should be practiced in four- and eight-measure forms as well. We'll start with a basic idea and then work on some orchestrations around the drumset. Use the same stickings for the orchestrations as the basic idea, unless otherwise indicated.

Basic Idea

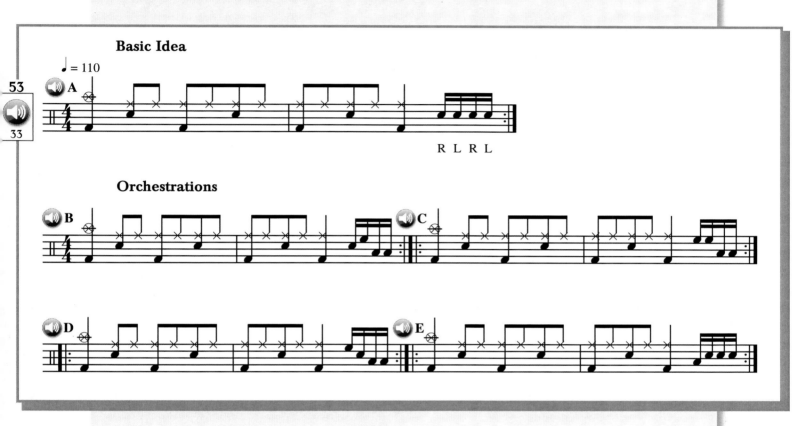

Orchestrations

Basic Idea

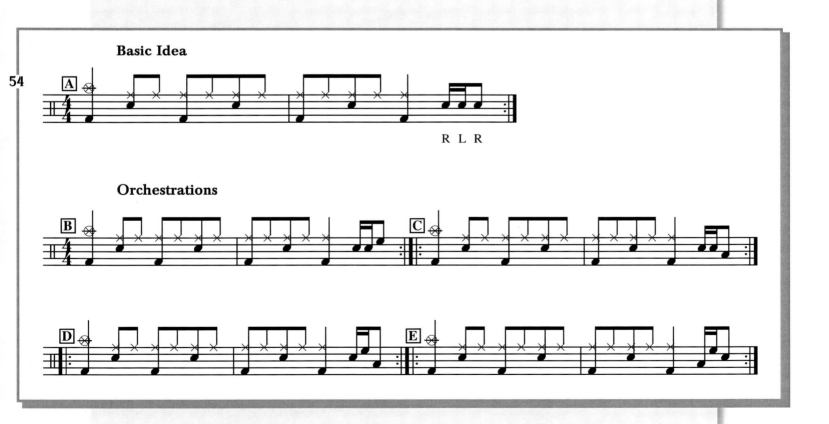

Orchestrations

55

Basic Idea

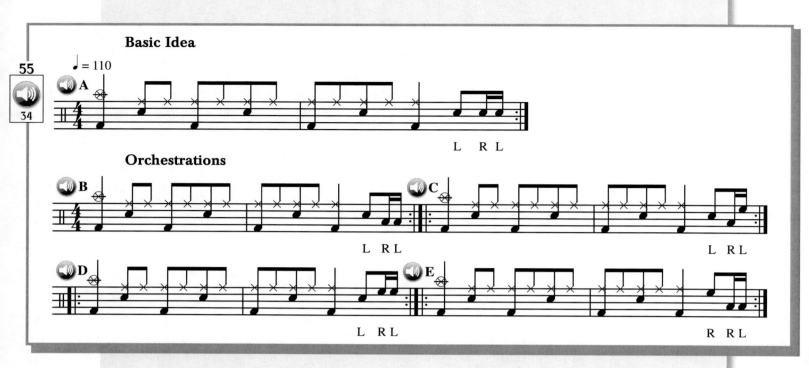

Orchestrations

Basic Idea

56

Orchestrations

Basic Idea

57

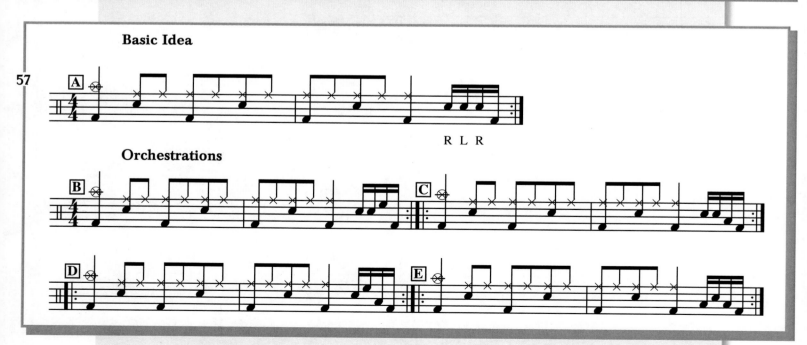

Orchestrations

Basic Idea

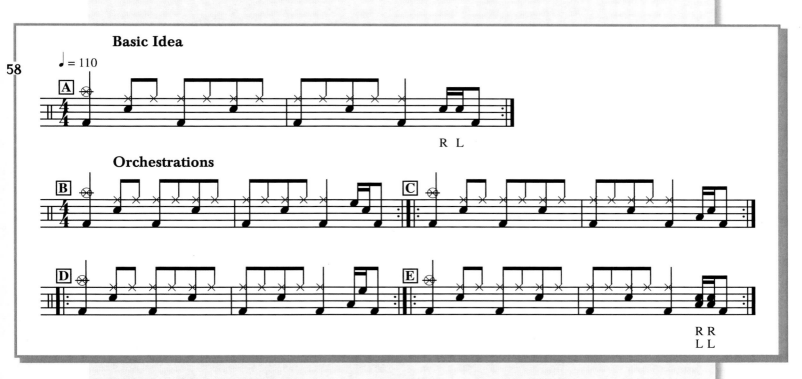

Orchestrations

Basic Idea

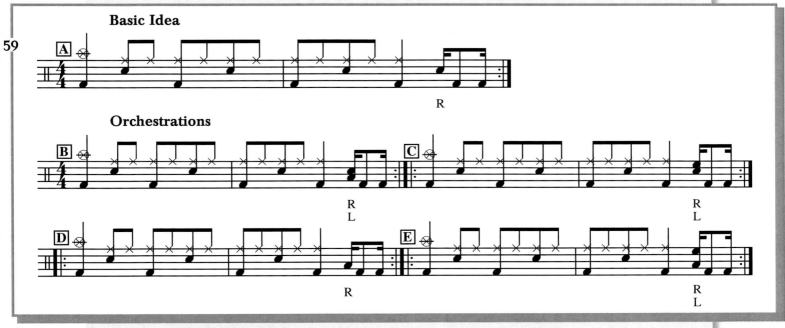

Orchestrations

Basic Idea

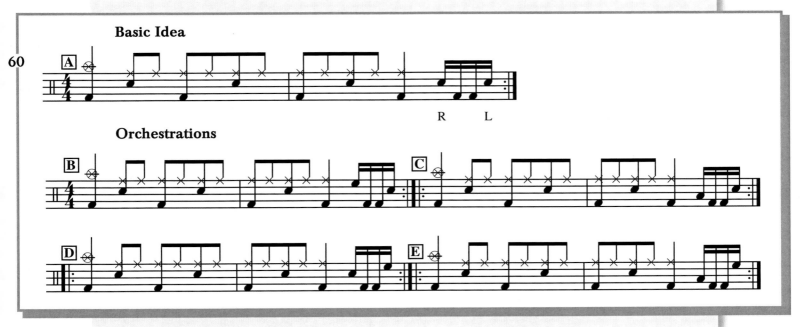

Orchestrations

TWO-BEAT SIXTEENTH-NOTE DRUM FILLS

Here are some sixteenth-note fills that are two beats in length. Again, we'll start off with a basic idea played on the snare drum and then apply it around the full set. (Remember to follow the stickings from the basic idea when playing the orchestrations.) Once you have the concept of the fill understood, take some time to come up with ideas of your own based on the basic phrase. Work on your own ways of orchestrating the fill around the set.

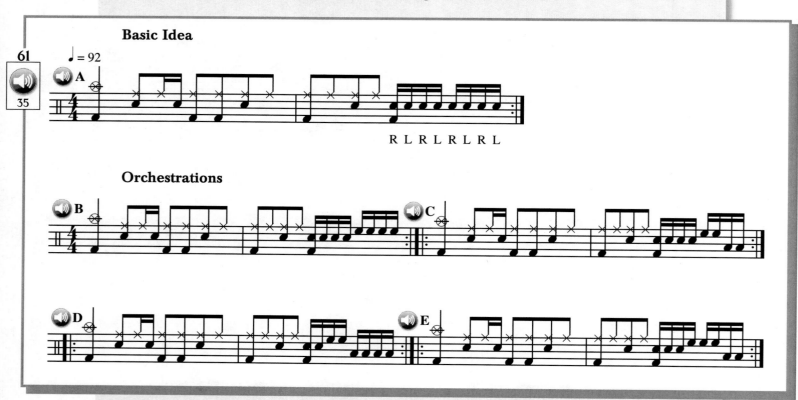

Basic Idea

Orchestrations

Basic Idea

Orchestrations

Basic Idea

Orchestrations

ADDITIONAL TWO-BEAT FILLS

The following examples will give you lots of ideas for drum fills in two beats of time. This is very useful when playing rock and funk music. Each example will be introduced on the snare drum, then followed by one orchestration on the set. Follow the indicated stickings. Each of these examples should be practiced as the end of a four-measure phrase: three measures of a groove, followed by one measure that has the two-beat fill.

Here are some more two-beat fills.

THREE-BEAT DRUM FILLS

The following examples will give you some ideas for playing fills in the time of three beats. We'll start out again working on an example and then move that basic idea around the drumset. Once you have learned the ideas and its variations, take some time and create your own orchestrations.

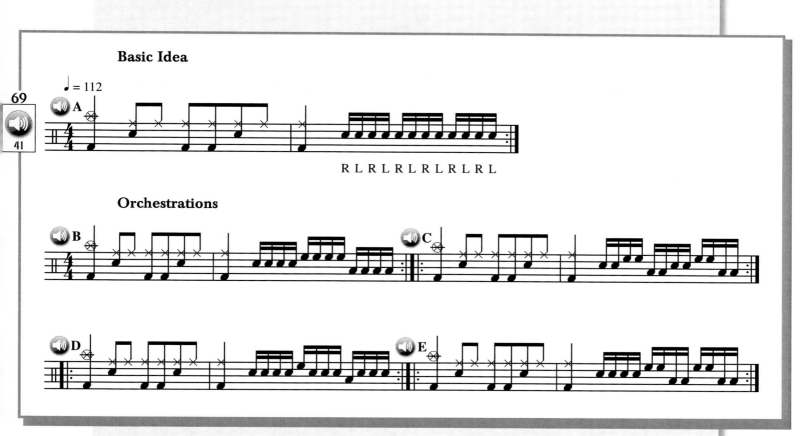

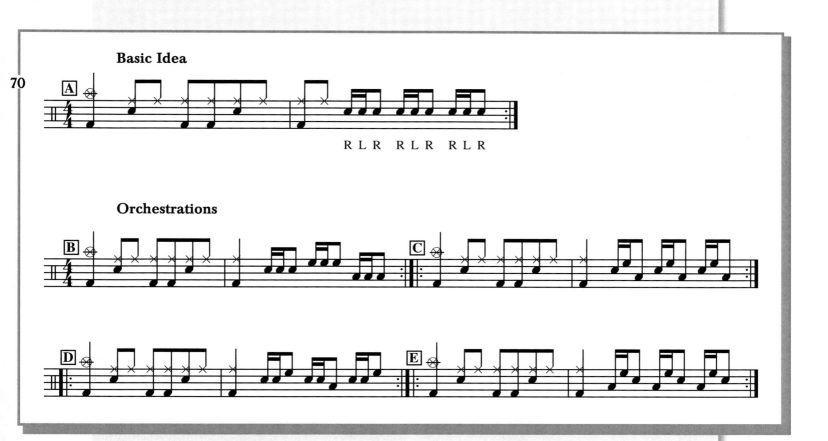

Basic Idea

Orchestrations

Basic Idea

Orchestrations

Basic Idea

Orchestrations

ADDITIONAL THREE-BEAT FILLS

The following examples will give you more three-beat fills to work on. Practice these by playing them in a four-bar structure: Three measures of a beat, then a fourth measure with the three-beat fill.

ONE-MEASURE DRUM FILLS

The next step will be to work on drum fills that are four beats or one measure in length. Make sure you count each beat as you play these fills so that the tempo stays steady and consistent.

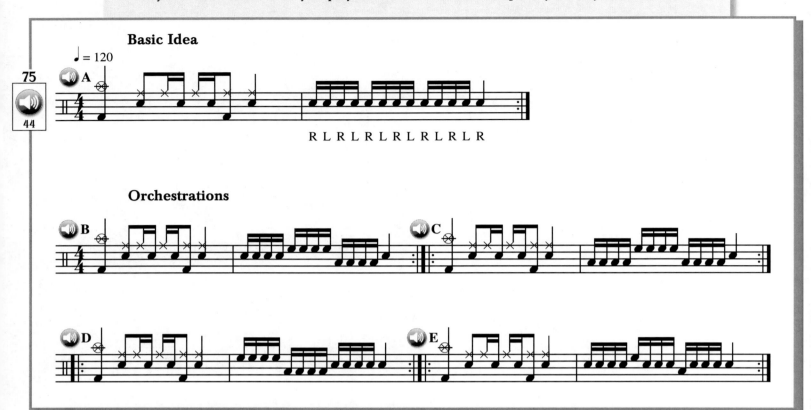

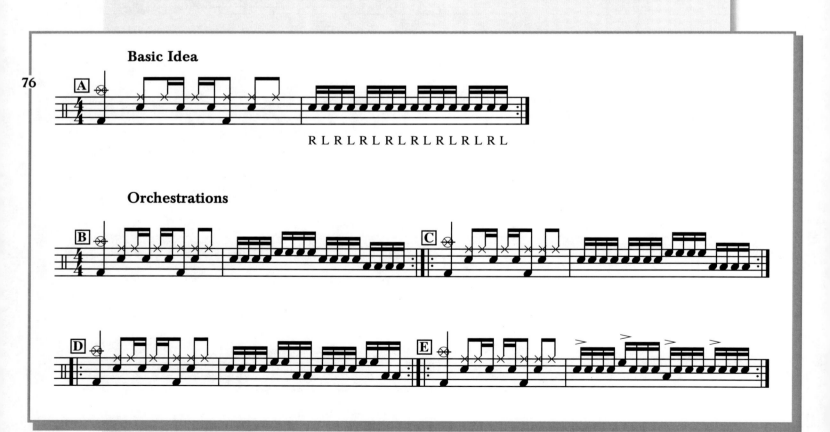

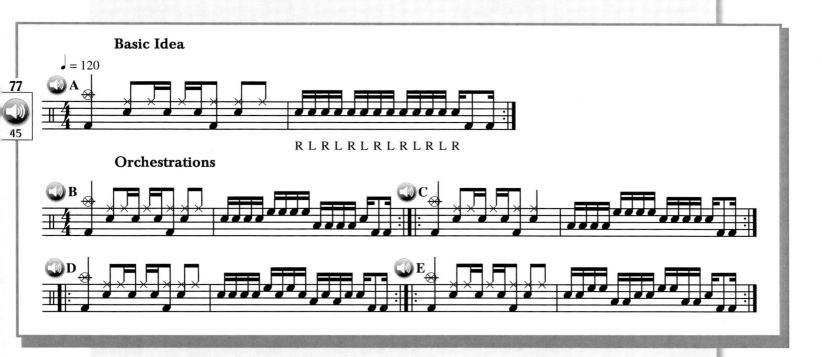

Basic Idea

Orchestrations

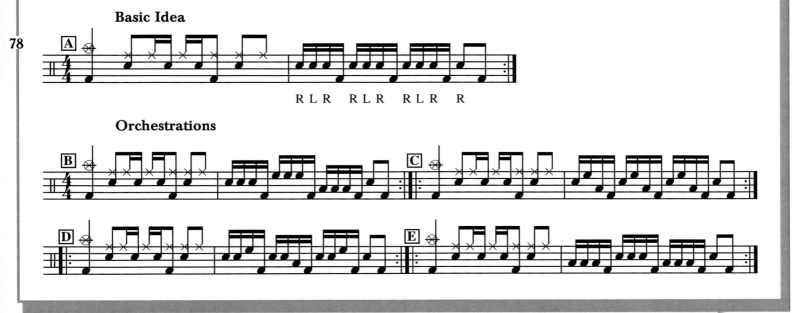

Basic Idea

Orchestrations

Basic Idea

Orchestrations

ADDITIONAL ONE-MEASURE FILLS

Work on these examples in a four-measure structure: three bars of a beat, followed by one measure of a fill. The basic idea will be initially introduced on snare, followed by three variations around the full drumset.

USING DRUM FILLS AS A PICKUP

Many songs begin with a short drum fill as an intro or *pickup*. The following examples will give you some ideas that are commonly used in funk and rock tunes. They are generally one or two beats in length and end, or *resolve*, with a crash on beat 1.

DRUM FILLS THAT RESOLVE ON AN UPBEAT

Up to now, the drum fills we have been working with resolve on beat 1. Many times, though, you will have to play fills that resolve on an upbeat, or "&," of beat 4. Notice that the crash and bass drum are tied over to beat 1. This means you should let the note ring out through beat 1.

You can end a fill with double hit on the crash. These fills end on the "&" of beat 4 and the downbeat of beat 1.

These fills end with crashes on the last sixteenth note of the measure and on beat 1 of the next measure.

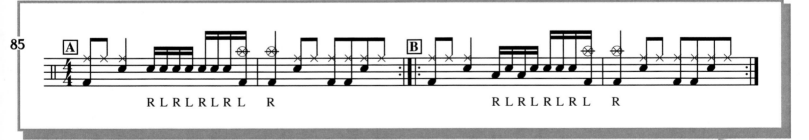

Here, we are resolving the drum fills on the very last sixteenth note of the measure. This gives the fill a very up-beat, *anticipated* feeling. Anticipation means playing a note slightly before it would normally be expected.

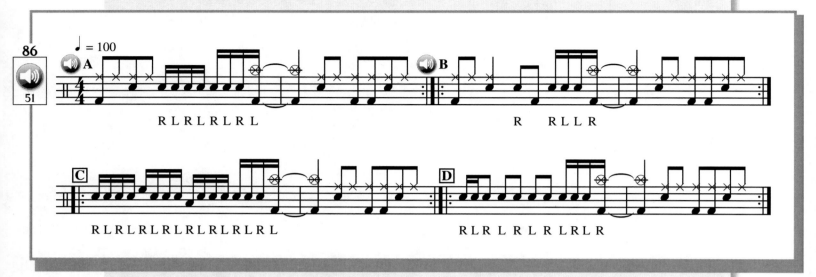

You can end fills on the last two sixteenths of the measure.

Sometimes, it sounds cool to end the fill later than beat 1. These next examples resolve on the "&" of beat 1 in the next measure.

It's also a different twist when you end a fill without crashing. These fills end with the snare hitting on beat 1.

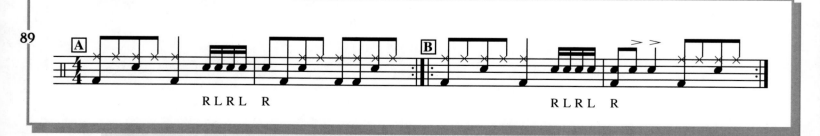

CHAPTER SIX
TRIPLET DRUM FILLS

Triplets are found in drum fills in many styles of music. You can hear triplets in blues, rock, reggae, funk, and jazz. Let's begin by reviewing what triplets are. A triplet is a group of three notes that fits into the duration normally occupied by two notes of the same value. The eighth-note triplets in the following examples consist of three notes per beat, instead of two regular or *straight* eighth notes. To get familiar with the eighth-note triplet, play the following exercise with a single-stroke roll sticking. Notice how the quarter note is played back and forth from the right hand to the left. Because triplets are an uneven note value, the lead hand shifts.

Now, play this in the context of a beat and fill: one measure of a beat, followed by one measure of triplets.

Following is an exercise to help get you more familiar with the eighth-note triplet. Play this with the bass drum on all four beats and the stepped hi-hat on beats 2 and 4.

TRIPLET READING EXERCISE

Below is a series of reading exercises to get you more familiar with the different ways an eighth-note triplet can be broken up. By using rests, the triplet can be made into some very interesting musical phrases. Recognizing these broken triplet rhythms is essential for playing the drum fills that will follow.

ONE-BEAT TRIPLET DRUM FILLS

Now, let's take some of the triplet rhythms you have been working on and apply them to drum fills. Make sure you pay strict attention to all of the stickings that are indicated.

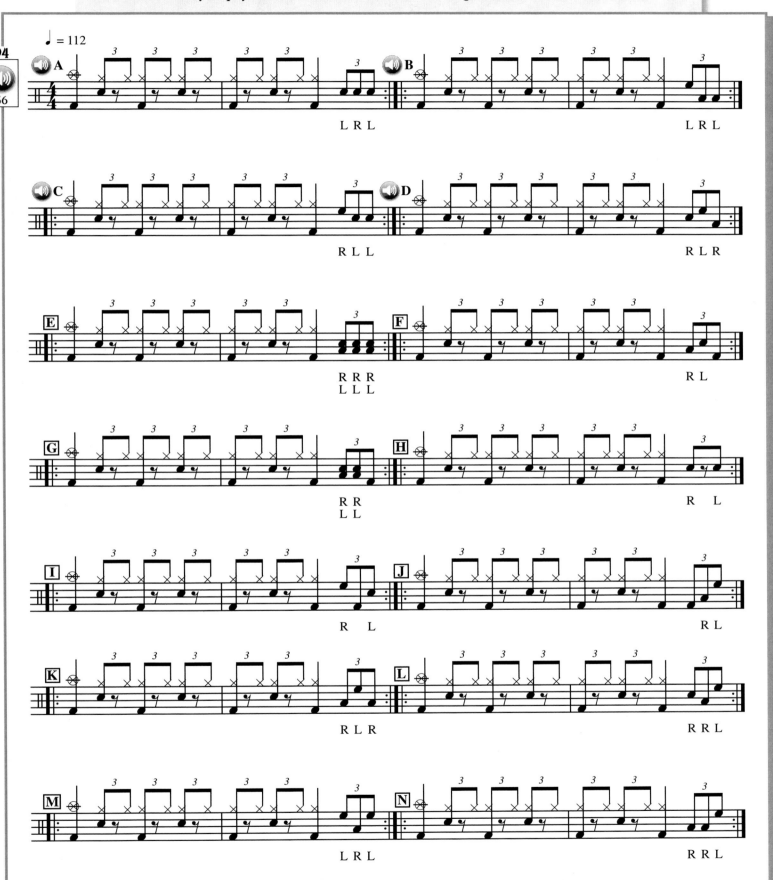

TWO-BEAT TRIPLET FILLS

The following series of examples will give you lots of ideas for triplet-based fills in the time of two beats. These can be adapted to rock, blues, or jazz settings and should be practiced at a variety of tempos.

Here are some more two-beat triplet fills for you to try.

THREE-BEAT TRIPLET FILLS

Practice all of these examples with the stickings that are indicated. Eventually, try experimenting with your own orchestrations and stickings around the drumset. These examples are meant to be starting points for your own creative explorations.

ONE-MEASURE TRIPLET FILLS

The following examples will have you playing fills in the time of four beats, or one whole measure. First, learn the fill idea and then practice it in a musical structure. You can play three measures of a beat and use the fill as your fourth measure. Have fun!

The next series of examples will have the bass drum utilized as a third hand. Practice these slowly at first to get the proper timing for each idea.

TRIPLET FILLS WITH FLAMS

A *flam* consists of a grace note before the principal note. A *single flam* looks like this:

Here are some applications of the single flam in fills.

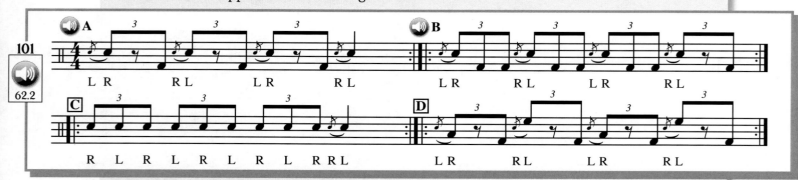

THE FLAM ACCENT

The *flam accent* is basically a single-stroke roll as triplets with a flam at the beginning of each triplet. Start with the single-stroke roll and then add the flams.

102
63.1

R L R L R L R L R L R L   L R L R R L R L L R L R R L R L

Here are some ways to use the flam accent as a fill.

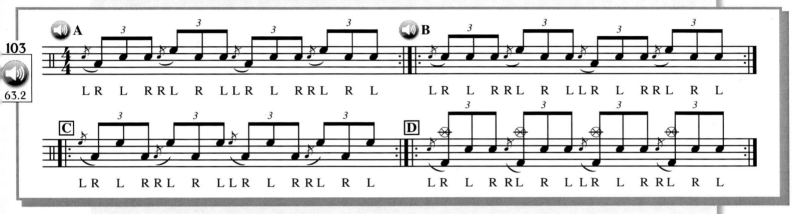

103
63.2

A
L R L R R L R L L R L R R L R L

B
L R L R R L R L L R L R R L R L

C
L R L R R L R L L R L R R L R L

D
L R L R R L R L L R L R R L R L

SWISS TRIPLETS

The *Swiss triplet* is a RRL RRL (or LLR LLR) sticking with a flam in the beginning of each double stroke. Start with the basic sticking and then add the flams.

104
64.1

A
R R L R R L R R L R R L   L R R L L R R L L R R L

B
L L R L L R L L R L L R   R L L R R L L R R L L R

Here are some fills using the Swiss triplet:

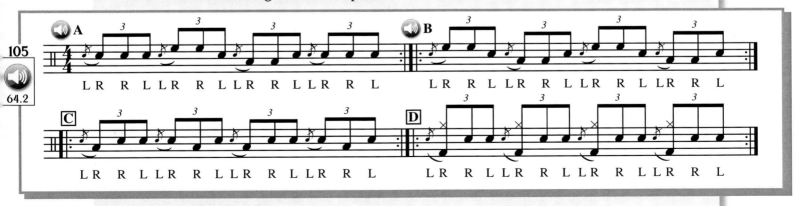

105
64.2

A
L R R L L R R L L R R L R L

B
L R R L L R R L L R R L R L

C
L R R L L R R L L R R L R L

D
L R R L L R R L L R R L R L

DIFFERENT FILL RESOLUTIONS

There are many ways to resolve fills in the triplet style. A very common way to end a fill is on the "&" of beat 4, which gives it an upbeat, anticipated feeling.

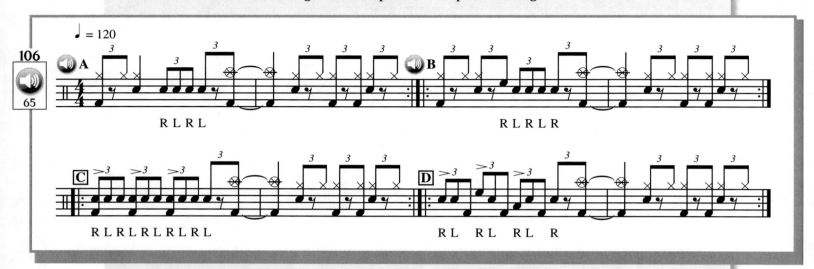

You can also double hit the "&" of beat 4 and the downbeat of beat 1.

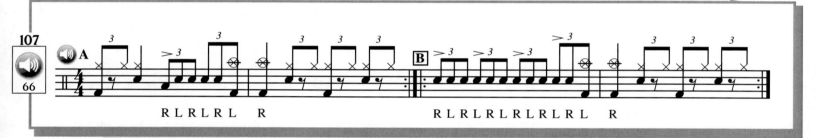

In the following example, the fill ends with the second and third note of the triplet.

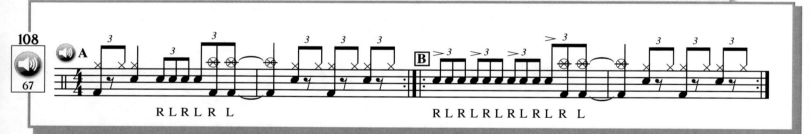

Here's another example with a triple hit of the second and third note of the triplet, followed by a final hit on the downbeat of beat 1.

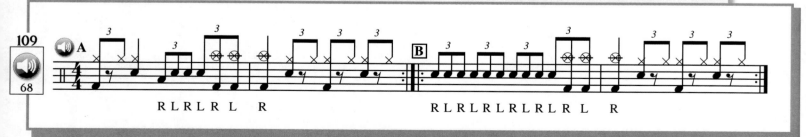

CHAPTER SEVEN
ADVANCED DRUM FILLS

In this chapter, we'll work on drum fills that use sixteenth-note triplets and thirty-second notes. You'll also learn many new and interesting ways to orchestrate your fills around the drumset. Let's get started!

SIXTEENTH-NOTE TRIPLETS

Sixteenth-note triplets are twice as fast as the eighth-note triplets we have been working on. The sixteenth-note triplet consists of six evenly spaced notes in the time of one beat. To get started, play eighth-note triplets with just your right hand. Accent the first note of each triplet.

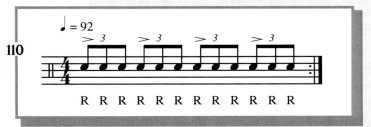

Now, fill in all of the offbeats with your left hand while still maintaining the eighth-note triplets with your right. Keep the accents going on every beat.

The following exercises will help you develop the ability to play great sounding sixteenth-note triplets with a single-stroke roll sticking. You will need this ability first before applying these triplets to drum fills. Play these examples slowly at first before playing them up to speed. Listen for accuracy!

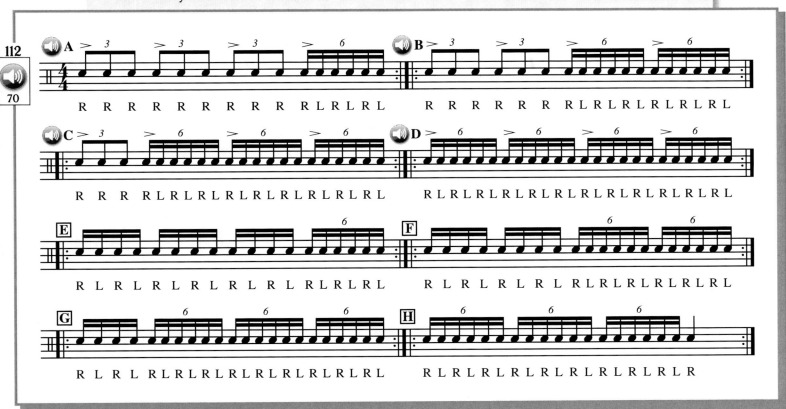

USING SIXTEENTH-NOTE TRIPLETS IN FILLS

Sixteenth-note triplets make great-sounding drum fills. Here are some short fills to get you started. All of these use the single-stroke roll sticking.

Now, let's apply the sixteenth-note triplet to some one-measure fills. Be sure to count the quarter-note pulse as you are playing these fills.

THE FOUR-STROKE RUFF

If you play three sixteenth-note triplets and an eighth note, you get a rhythm called the *four-stroke ruff.* This is a cool-sounding idea that can be used on the drumset in lots of different ways. There are two basic ways to play the four-stroke ruff: on the beat or off the beat. It may help to think of the rhythm initially in half-time as an eighth-note triplet and a quarter note.

On the beat:

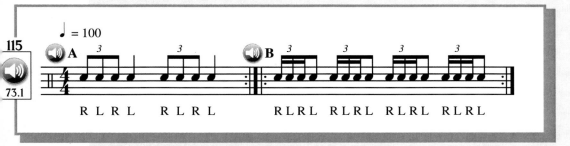

Off the beat:

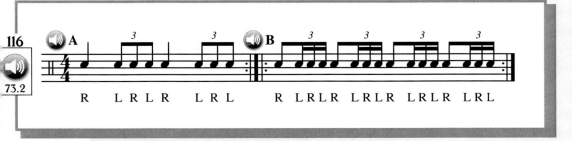

Let's apply the four-stroke ruff to some drum fills.

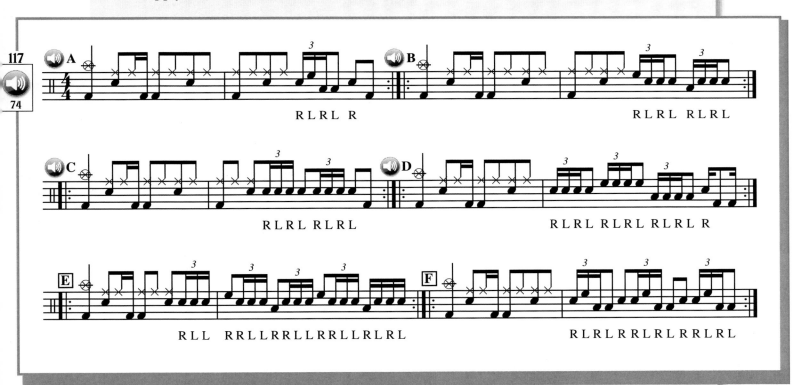

If you replace the last note of the ruff with the bass drum, you get a great sounding drum fill.

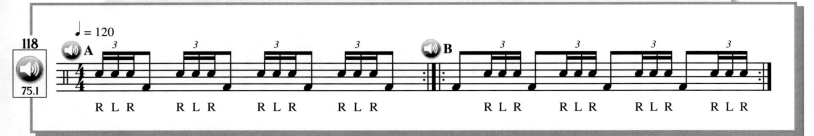

Here's the phrase from above used in some drum fills.

SHORT SIXTEENTH-NOTE TRIPLET RIFFS

Here are some great fill ideas that combine sixteenth-note triplets and eighth-note triplets.
The basic hand patterns are as follows:

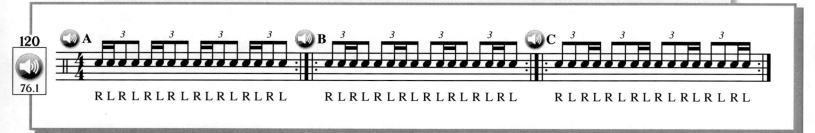

And now, applied to some drum fills:

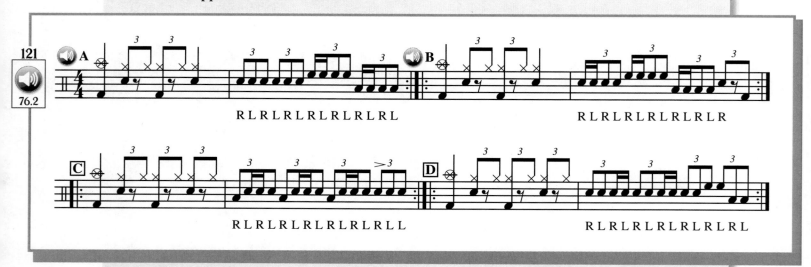

THE SIX-STROKE ROLL

The six-stroke roll is a very common and useful way to play drum fills and solos. First, you will need to practice the basic sticking patterns before using them at the set. Here are four variations for you to work on. Make sure all of the single and double strokes flow well.

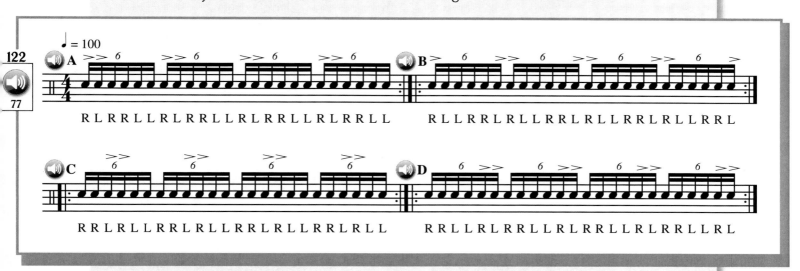

Now, let's take these six-stroke rolls and use them on the set. Learn these patterns first and then spend time coming up with variations of your own. The possibilities are endless!

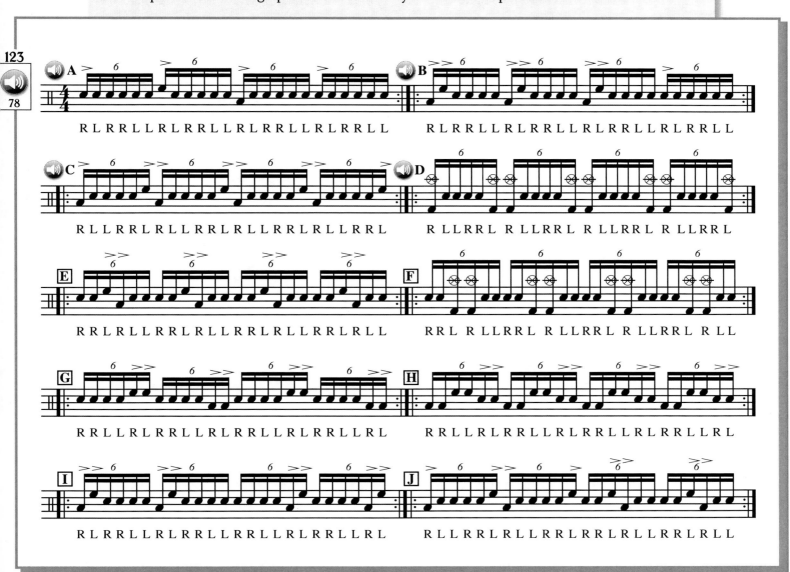

HAND AND FOOT FILLS USING SIXTEENTH-NOTE TRIPLETS

One of the most interesting ways to use sixteenth-note triplets is to play them as hand and foot patterns. These make great sounding solos and fills and are a challenge to play. You can hear rock drummers like John Bonham of Led Zeppelin or fusion drummers like Steve Gadd and Dave Weckl use these types of phrases on the drumset. Use these examples as one-measure fills.

THIRTY-SECOND NOTES

To get started with thirty-second notes, let's begin by looking at their relationship to sixteenth notes. Thirty-second notes are twice as fast as sixteenth notes. You can think of them as eight evenly-spaced notes in the time of one beat. You can work on the transition from sixteenths to thirty-seconds by first playing sixteenths continuously with your right hand. Now, fill in all of the offbeats with your left hand, and you have thirty-second notes.

125
80.1

R R R R R R R R R R R R R R R R R L R L R L R L R L R L R L R L R L R L R L R L R L R L

Practice going from sixteenths to thirty-seconds until you feel very comfortable and relaxed with the transition. This will more than likely be easier at slower tempos. The next series of exercises will help you become more familiar with thirty-second notes in short phrases, which is how they are commonly used in drum fills. Play these with a single-stroke roll sticking.

126
80.2

A
R L R L R L R L R L R L R L R L R L R L R L

B
R L R L R L R L R L R L R L R L R L R L R L R L

C
R L R L R L R L R L R L R L R L R L R L R L R L R L R L

D
R L R L R L R L R L R L R L R L R L R L R L R L R L R L R L R L

SIX-STROKE ROLL AS THIRTY-SECOND NOTES

The six-stroke roll you worked on as triplets can also be used in thirty-second note patterns. Here are the basic stickings.

127
81

A
R L R L R L R L R L R L R L R L R L R L R L R L

B
R L R L R L R L R L R L R L R L R L R L R L R L

APPLYING THIRTY-SECOND NOTES TO DRUM FILLS

The fun really begins when you start using these thirty-second notes around the drumset. They make very cool drum fills that give excitement to the music. All of these fills should be played with a single-stroke roll sticking.

THIRTY-SECOND NOTE DOUBLE-STROKE ROLL

Another way to play thirty-second notes is to use the double-stroke roll. This is accomplished by first playing sixteenth notes with a single-stroke roll sticking, and then doubling each of those strokes to make thirty-second notes.

129
83.1

R L R L R L R L R L R L R L R L   R R L L R R L L R R L L R R L L R R L L R R L L R R L L R R L L

Following is an exercise to develop your double-stroke roll abilities. These strokes are to be played *open*, which means that each double is two distinct notes. They are not *buzzed* or *closed*, which means multiple-bounce strokes.

130
83.2

A   R L R L R L R L R L R L R L R L R R L L

B   R L R L R L R L R L R L R L R L R R L L R R L L

C   R L R L R L R L R L R R L L R R L L R R L L

D   R L R L R L R L R R L L R R L L R R L L R R L L

E   R L R L R L R R L L R R L L R R L L R R L L R R L L

F   R L R L R R L L R R L L R R L L R R L L R R L L R R L L

G   R L R R L L R R L L R R L L R R L L R R L L R R L L

H   R R L L R R L L R R L L R R L L R R L L R R L L R R L L

SHORT PHRASES USING DOUBLES

These are short fill ideas that are basically a double stroke here and there. Make sure each of these doubles sounds strong.

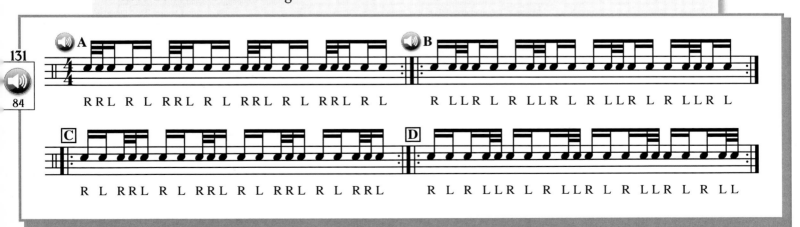

131
84

A   R R L   R L   R R L   R L   R R L   R L   R R L   R L

B   R L L R   L R   L L R   L R   L L R   L R   L L R   L

C   R L   R R L   R L   R R L   R L   R R L   R L   R R L

D   R L R   L L R   L R   L L R   L R   L L R   L R L L

THE SIX-STROKE ROLL AS THIRTY-SECOND NOTE DOUBLES

A very common way to play thirty-second notes is to apply them to the six-stroke roll. Here are your basic variations.

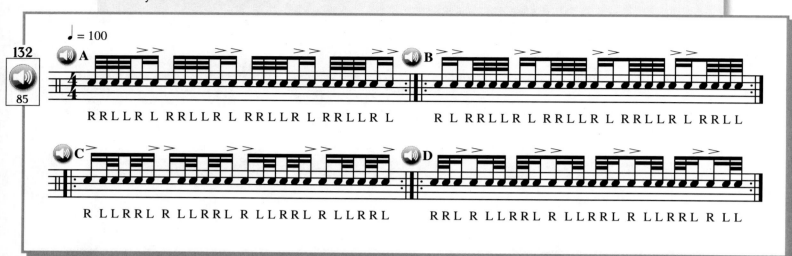

Now, let's apply some of the short rolls and six-stroke rolls to drum fills. These fills sound great in many different styles of music. They are useful in rock, funk, hip-hop, and progressive rock situations.

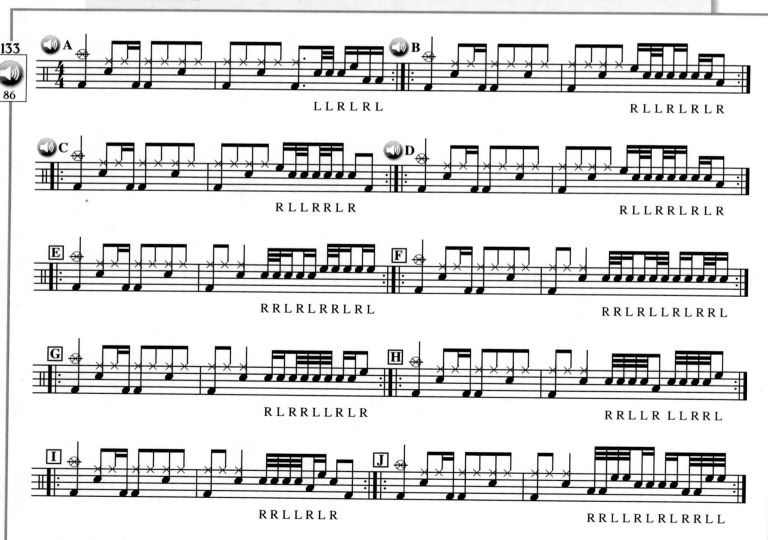

MORE THIRTY-SECOND NOTE FILLS

There are lots of ways to use thirty-second note fills at the drumset. Here are some examples that will utilize all of the skills you have learned regarding thirty-second notes. Notice that some of these fills have double thirty-second notes on the bass drum. Have fun with these ideas!

JAZZ FILLS WITH SIXTEENTH-NOTE TRIPLETS

A great way to play fills in the jazz style is to take eighth-note triplets and double them, making them sixteenth-note triplets with a double-stroke roll. In this first example, play eighth-note triplets with a single-stroke roll, then turn them into sixteenth-note triplets by doubling each stroke.

You can play five-stroke rolls this way, on or off the beat. They also work great for seven-stroke rolls. You can hear lots of examples of this in the playing of Buddy Rich or Philly Joe Jones.

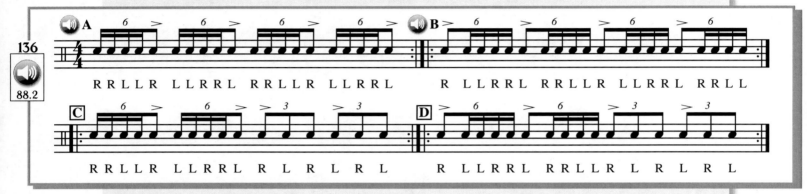

These sixteenth-note triplet ideas sound great when you apply them to hand and foot patterns at the set. Listen to Elvin Jones to hear these kinds of ideas being played as solos and fills.

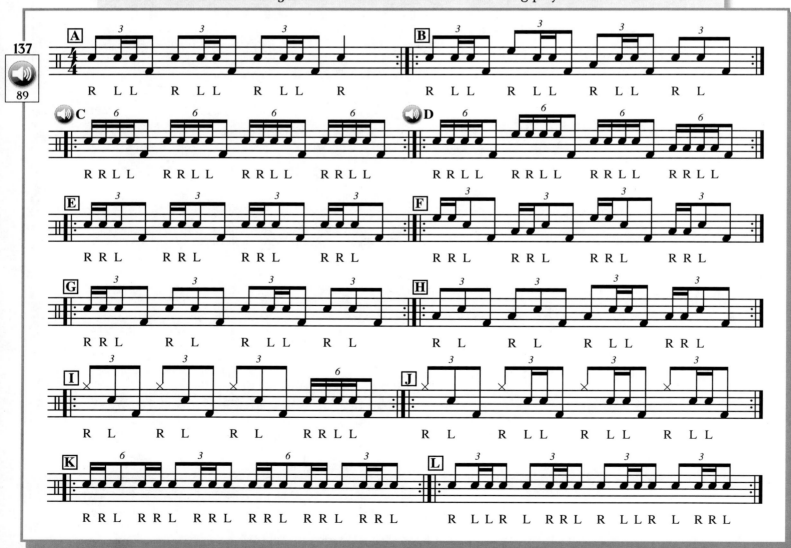

FILLS USING ODD NOTE GROUPINGS

In the next series of examples, we'll look at fills with sixteenth notes in odd-numbered groupings. The first odd grouping we'll work on is sixteenths in groups of three. To get started, play this accent pattern with a single-stroke roll sticking. Notice how it takes three whole measures to come back to beat 1 with the pattern.

138

♩ = 92

RLRLRLRLRLRLRLRL RLRLRLRLRLRLRLRL RLRLRLRLRLRLRLRL RLRLRLRLRLRLRLRL

If we apply this to a few sticking ideas, it will look like this:

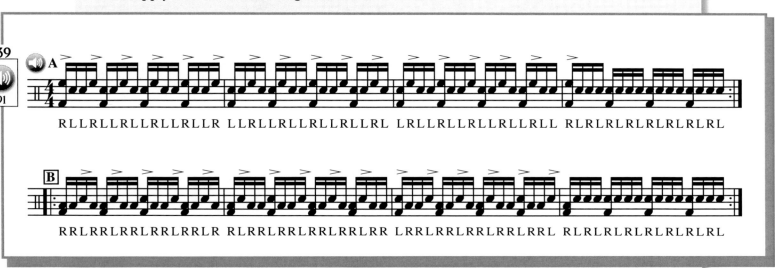

139

A

RLLRLLRLLRLLRLLR LLRLLRLLRLLRLLRL LRLLRLLRLLRLLRLL RLRLRLRLRLRLRLRL

B

RLRRLRRLRRLRRLRR RLRRLRRLRRLRRLRR LRRLRRLRRLRRLRRL RLRLRLRLRLRLRLRL

The phrasing of a three-note pattern essentially goes "over the barline," which means it doesn't resolve on beat 1 right away. Let's take this idea and apply it to some hand and foot patterns in a two-measure structure. Make sure you count each beat so you don't get lost! Note that the final example in this series is not technically a three-note pattern; it is the first example with the snare hits doubled to thirty-second notes.

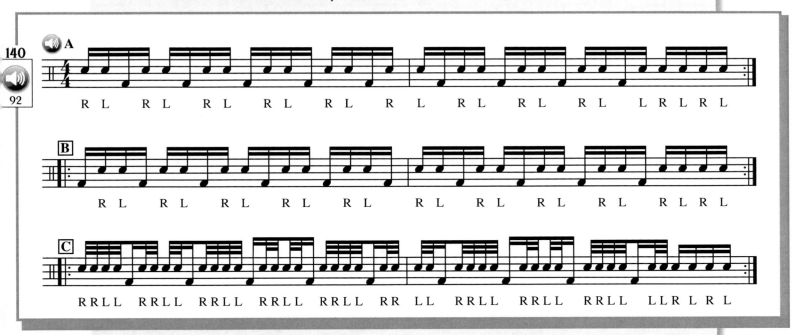

140

A

RL   RL   RL   RL   RL   RL   RL   RL   RL   LRLRL

B

RL   RL   RL   RL   RL   RL   RL   RL   RLRL

C

RRLL   RRLL   RRLL   RRLL   RRLL   RR   LL   RRLL   RRLL   RRLL   LLRLRL

GROUPS OF FIVE

We can use the same idea to create fills using groups of fives. First, play this accented hand pattern to hear how the fives fall into the time.

Now, apply the fives to some stickings. We'll do this in two-measure structures. The accents demonstrate a common approach to groups of five, which is to subdivide them into groups of two and three.

Here are the groups of fives used as hand and foot patterns at the drumset.

MIXING THE GROUPS OF THREES AND FIVES

By combining groups of threes and fives you can come up with some very interesting and musical-sounding fills and solos. Here are some one-measure ideas to get you started.

TWO-MEASURE IDEAS

You can combine these ideas to form two-measure fills and solos.

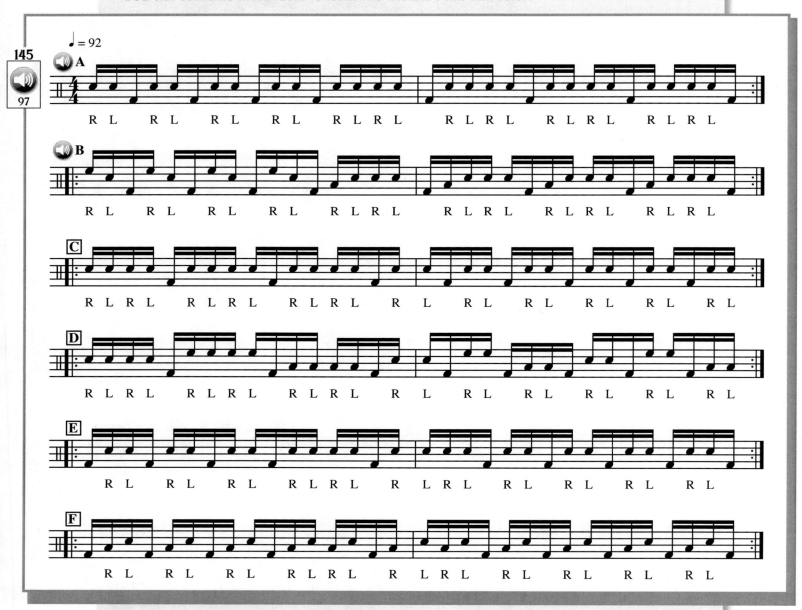

THE CREATIVE PROCESS

One of the most enjoyable elements of playing music is finding new ways to be creative. Try to devote some of your practice time each day to taking some basic ideas and really exploring how many different ways you can use them musically at the drumset. The following exercises are a starting point. First, learn the basic patterns with the stickings.

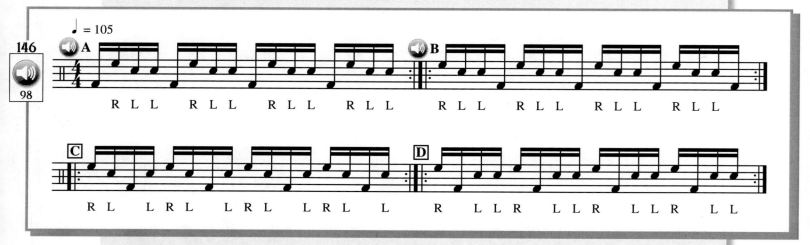

Now, take some of the patterns and combine them. For example, play two beats of the first example and two beats of the second example.

Or take one beat of the first and second examples:

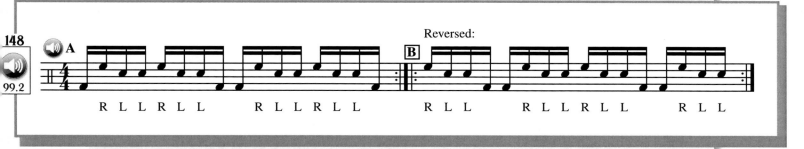

Or you can take one beat of the first example and three beats of the second example:

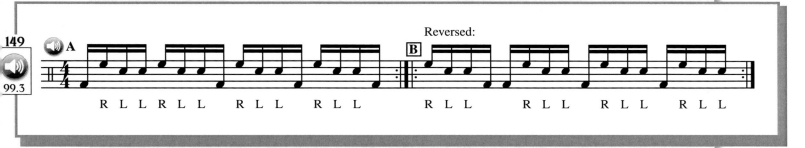

The possibilities are virtually endless when you apply your creativity to even basic ideas.

CONCLUSION

This concludes the *Drummer's Guide to Fills.* With the tools and vocabulary you've learned, you should be able to create interesting fills in just about any musical situation. The most important thing is to keep a steady groove, counting if necessary, so that your fills resolve on the correct beat. Mastering this skill will allow you the freedom to play the fill of your choice, whether simple or complex, with confidence.